Martin Luther King Jr. Day

Mir Tamim Ansary

Heinemann Library
Des Plaines, Illinois

Published by Heinemann Library,
an imprint of Reed Educational & Professional Publishing,
1350 East Touhy Avenue, Suite 240 West
Des Plaines, IL 60018

Printed in Hong Kong / China

03 02 01 00 99
10 9 8 7 6 5 4 3 2 1

Library of Congress Cataloging-in-Publication Data

Ansary, Mir Tamim, 1954-
    Martin Luther King Jr. Day / Mir Tamim Ansary.
        p.   cm. — (Holiday histories)
    Includes bibliographical references and index.
    Summary: Introduces Martin Luther King, Jr., Day, explaining the historical events behind it, how it became a holiday, and how it is observed.
    ISBN 1-57572-873-7 (lib. bdg.)
    1. Martin Luther King, Jr., Day—Juvenile literature. 2. King, Martin Luther, Jr., 1929-1968—Juvenile literature. [1. Martin Luther King, Jr., Day. 2. King, Martin Luther, Jr., 1929-1968. 3. Civil rights workers. 4. Clergy. 5. Afro-Americans—Biography. 6. Holidays.] I. Title. II. Series: Ansary, Mir Tamim. Holiday histories.
E185.97.K5A78   1998
394.261—dc21   98-14378
ANSARY   1489258   CIP
                                                                   AC

Acknowledgments
The publisher would like to thank the following for permission to reproduce photographs:

Cover: Photo Researchers, Inc./Thomas Hollyman

The Picture Cube, Inc./Eunice Harms, p. 4; Photo Researchers, Inc./Thomas Hollyman, p. 7; Corbis-Bettmann, pp. 8(left), 11(top), 22 (center); The Granger Collection, pp. 8(center), 10; UPI/Corbis-Bettmann, pp. 9, 11(bottom), 15, 16, 19, 20, 21; Life Magazine/Howard Sochurek, p. 12; AP/Wide World, pp. 13, 14, 17, 18, 22(left), 25, 26(all); Black Star/Charles Moore, p. 24; Photo Edit/Myrleen Ferguson, p. 28; Photo Edit/Nancy Sheehan, p. 29.

Some words are shown in bold, **like this**. You can find out what they mean by looking in the glossary.

Contents

A New Holiday

These children are very happy! They are starting a long weekend. Monday is Martin Luther King Jr. Day. Schools will be closed.

Martin Luther King Jr. Day is America's
newest holiday. It was celebrated across
the country for the first time in 1986. It
honors a great American.

Dr. Martin Luther King Jr.

Dr. Martin Luther King Jr. was not a president or a general. He didn't start a new religion. But he gave our country something wonderful.

He gave us a dream. To understand this dream, you have to know about things that happened in our country long ago.

Slavery and the Civil War

Long ago, African Americans were **slaves**. The **Civil War** set them free. But they did not get **equal rights**.

They were not allowed to vote in many
places. They could not get good jobs. Many
people disliked them because they had
darker skin.

New Laws

Some states passed laws to keep African Americans apart from other people. This was called segregation. African American people could not eat in the same restaurants as white people.

African American people could not marry
white people. They could not sit in the same
parts of a bus as white people. They even
had to go to separate schools.

★

From Boy to Man

Martin Luther King Jr. grew up with segregation. He was born in Atlanta, Georgia, in 1929. He wanted to change many things. But he didn't want to hurt anyone.

He had deep religious feelings. After college,
he became a **minister** in Montgomery,
Alabama. He also began studying the wisdom
of Mohandas Gandhi.

13

The Wisdom of Gandhi

Gandhi was an Indian teacher and leader. He believed the world could be changed without **violence**. He told his followers to meet hate with love.

Gandhi said people should not obey unfair laws. But they should not fight either. Dr. King wanted to try this peaceful way of pushing for change.

Rosa Parks Says No

In Alabama, the law said African American people had to sit in the back of the bus. One day in 1955, a woman named Rosa Parks said no to this. The police arrested her.

Dr. King said the law was wrong. He asked people to stop riding buses. The bus company started losing money. Sure enough, the law was changed.

The Lunch Counter Sit-In

Then four African American students sat at a white people's lunch counter in Greensboro, North Carolina. No one served them. Some people called them names. But they kept sitting there for four days! Some people sat with the students to show their **support**.

Dr. King led a **march** to cheer for these
students. Soon, African Americans stopped
obeying segregation laws in many cities.
Dr. King was arrested for giving them
the idea.

★

A Letter from Jail

Dr. King wrote to newspapers. He explained why he was leading **marches** against segregation. He said all Americans should have the same rights.

Thousands of people agreed with him. They too began to march. Even children joined these marches. Alabama sheriff Bull Connors put many of these children in jail.

Dr. King's Dream

In 1963, Dr. King led a **march** to Washington, D.C. There he gave his greatest speech. He told people of his dream.

★

He said he dreamed of a world that was fair. People of all colors lived together in peace. A crowd of 250 thousand people heard him and began to dream, too.

★
23

Meeting Hate with Love

The dream spread across America. Millions of people began working for **equal rights**. Sometimes police beat them up, but they never fought back.

They followed Dr. King's rule—meet hate with love. It worked. Slowly, segregation ended. In 1964, new laws were passed. They promised equal rights to all Americans.

President Lyndon Johnson signs the Civil Rights Act of 1964.

The Death of Dr. King

Four years later, in 1968, a man shot Dr. King. Millions of people cried. What would happen to Dr. King's dream? Had the bullet killed that, too?

Dr. King was buried. Four days later, Senator John Conyers of Michigan had an idea: America should have a holiday to **honor** Martin Luther King Jr.

Remembering the Dream

Martin Luther King Day Jr. began in 1983. It is on the third Monday of January. People across the country get together to remember Dr. King's dream.

It's a good day to start living the dream, too. It's a good day to reach out and make new friends.

Important Dates

Martin Luther King Jr. Day

1518	African slave trade begins
1865	The Civil War ends slavery in the United States
1865–1900	Southern states pass segregation laws
1929	Martin Luther King Jr. is born
1954	Dr. King becomes a minister
1955	Rosa Parks sparks the Montgomery, Alabama, bus **boycott**
1960	Black students in Greensboro, North Carolina stage a sit-in
1963	Dr. King is arrested in Birmingham, Alabama
1963	Dr. King gives his greatest speech in Washington, D.C.
1964	The Civil Rights Act is passed
1965	The Voting Rights Act is passed
1968	Dr. King is killed
1983	Congress declares Martin Luther King Jr. Day
1986	Martin Luther King Jr. Day is celebrated nationwide

Glossary

boycott to join together to stop buying or using a product or service

Civil War American war (1861–1865) between the Northern states and the Southern states

equal rights when everyone is treated the same

honors shows respect for someone

march many people walking to show their strong belief in something

minister leader of a church

segregation laws that separate people of different skin colors

slaves people who were forced to work for other people and were owned, bought, and sold like property

speech talk given to a crowd of people

support to help or agree with someone

violence to use force to get something

More Books to Read

Lowery, Linda. *Martin Luther King Day.* Minneapolis, Minn: Lerner Publishing Group, 1987.

MacMillan, Diane. *Martin Luther King, Jr.* Springfield, NJ: Enslow Publishers, 1992.

Roop, Peter and Connie. *Martin Luther King Jr.* Des Plaines, Ill: Heinemann Library, 1997.

Index